# Waterfront Homes

*from Castles to Cottages*

# Waterfront Homes

*from Castles to Cottages*

E. Ashley Rooney

4880 Lower Valley Road, Atglen, PA 19310 USA

**Photo Credits:**

*Front cover photos: Center:* Courtesy of © John Bellenis, Photography; *Top Right:* Courtesy of @ Anton Grassl Photography; *Bottom Right:* Courtesy of D. Peter Lund

*Back cover photos: Top:* Courtesy of Topsider; *Bottom:* Courtesy of @ Anton Grassl Photography; *Insets (clockwise from top):* Courtesy of R. W. Green; Courtesy of Hope Zimmerman AIA; Courtesy of Arthur Cotton Moore FAIA

*Half title page photo:* Courtesy of Art Hupey
*Frontispiece photo:* Courtesy of D. Peter Lund
*Title page photo:* Courtesy of Topsider
*Spine photo:* Courtesy of Zaik/Miller Associates

Courtesy of Topsider.

Library of Congress Cataloging-in-Publication Data

Rooney, E. Ashley.
  Waterfront homes: from castles to cottages/ by E. Ashley Rooney.
    p. cm.
  ISBN 0-7643-1893-4
1. Seaside architecture. I. Title.
NA7574.R66 2003
728'.0914'6—dc21
                                        2003012470

Designed by John P. Cheek
Cover design by Bruce Waters
Type set in Adobe Jensen Regular/Humanist 521 BT

ISBN: 0-7643-1893-4
Printed in China

Published by Schiffer Publishing Ltd.
4880 Lower Valley Road
Atglen, PA 19310
Phone: (610) 593-1777; Fax: (610) 593-2002
E-mail: Info@schifferbooks.com
Please visit our web site catalog at **www.schifferbooks.com**
We are always looking for people to write books on new and related subjects.
If you have an idea for a book, please contact us at the above address.

This book may be purchased from the publisher.
Include $3.95 for shipping.
Please try your bookstore first.
You may write for a free catalog.

In Europe, Schiffer books are distributed by
Bushwood Books
6 Marksbury Avenue
Kew Gardens
Surrey TW9 4JF England
Phone: 44 (0) 20 8392 8585
Fax: 44 (0) 20 8392 9876
E-mail: Bushwd@aol.com
Free postage in the UK. Europe: air mail at cost.

# Contents

*Courtesy of Don Ritz, Architect*

# Acknowledgments

This book on waterfront homes would not have been done if my father, Stanley C. Schuler, a well-known writer on many subjects, had not told Peter Schiffer that I would write a book on kitchen collectibles. Perhaps he was like the wise king in one of those fairy tales, setting me on a new path.

But a book on kitchen collectibles was not the path for me. I only knew how to use the utensils – not to collect them.

My editor, Tina Skinner, who has guided this entire process, suggested that waterfront homes might be more in my purview. With that suggestion, I knew that she would be a good and wise guide in undertaking a book on waterfront homes.

So Peter Lund, my husband, and I began a new passage in our lives together. He would do the photography and I the writing. Together, we would find those waterfront homes.

We had a wonderful summer visiting the best of waterfront properties, enjoying our friends, and meeting some new ones.

My dad introduced us to other remarkable homeowners who were willing to share their stories and their beautiful homes. It was a grand opportunity to understand more about Americans and what drives us in our pursuit for a home. Ultimately, fourteen gracious homeowners let us photograph their homes. We thank them.

Still the task was overwhelming, until Jonathan Isleib from Interdesign Limited (Old Lyme, Connecticut) sent his architectural photos. He was the catalyst for my realization that I could approach architects, like him, who could be great sources of wisdom.

Subsequently, I "met" over the Internet many architects and builders who had fascinating approaches to designing a home on the waterfront. I began to know them through their work.

My one remaining concern was how to organize the book. Clay Benjamin Smook AIA (North Quincy, Massachusetts) gave me some advice that helped me in categorizing these seventy homes. Later, I asked him if he would be willing to write a Foreword on "Dreaming, Designing, and Living a Waterfront Life." His subsequent essay is a delight.

Every writer needs a good friend who makes her laugh and listens to her air her concerns. Peter has been my good friend throughout this process. He, my father, and towards the end my sister, Cary Hull, were there, listening, advising, guiding.

Most of all, I must acknowledge these homes. Each is lovely. Each frames the water in its own unique way. Each is a dream that has been transformed into reality.

*Courtesy of D. Peter Lund*

# Introduction

I grew up on Long Island Sound in an area of rivers, ponds, and brooks. Like many children, I played in the brooks, damming them, sending small boats down them, looking for fish and waterbugs, dropping pebbles in the water, and watching the ripples circling on and on and on.

There is something wonderful about living on the water.

Many of us dream about having a house there. Some want to live on the edge of uncertainty at the ocean's edge. Others want the gentle lapping of a lake; some want the gurgle of a stream.

The United States certainly has many beautiful waterfront sites. They range from our rivers, to the many lakes, ponds, brooks, and oceans. Native Americans and the early settlers looked to them for sustenance.

Today, many of these sites are seen as tourist attractions. They are found alongside quaint villages with mom-and-pop restaurants, upscale boutiques, and scenic drives. Some can be found within urban settings rich with cultural activities and recreational challenges. Still others can be found among deep forests, open meadows, and great cliffs.

This book presents many waterfront homes. There are castles and cottages, cliffhangers, communities, and some in between. Many are described by their architects, so you can visualize them through the designer's eyes and the camera.

Others are described as we saw them. In finding these homes, we talked to their owners about their feelings. Many people mentioned the beauty of living on the water: from the first tender green days of spring when pastel blooms painted the hills to those warm June days when boats of all sizes and types filled the waterways, to the cool crisp days of fall when the land blazed red, gold, and orange.

When winter comes and snowflakes fall into the murmuring water, life on the water changes. People leave, and the land becomes quiet again with only the snapping, crackling ice punctuating the cold. New animals appear, and the chimney smoke settles into the valleys.

Most owners of waterfront homes study nature, love nature, and feel close to nature. They mention the joys of watching the loons, the ospreys, the herons, the ducks, the deer, the fox, and even the seals.

Living on the water, beyond the confusion of life, can bring us into rhythm with nature. It seemingly helps us know where we belong. It restores us – makes us feel whole again.

Our dream houses can be modest or opulent, simple or complex, open or closed. They need to relate to and not be overpowered by the water. They need to stand up to the power of the water and the wind – to respect the richness of life on the water without overwhelming it.

The intent of this book is to allow you to dream about your waterfront home.

*Courtesy of R. W. Green*

# Foreword

## Dreaming, Designing, and Living a Waterfront Life

The lure of waterfront living has endured for centuries. Originally, cities and towns were located along shorelines – not for reasons of leisure but for more pragmatic reasons: sustenance, trade, and defense. Today many people enjoy coastline habitation as a life choice.

For a great many of us, the notion of living waterside conjures up images of a castle on the Rhine, a palazzo on the Grand Canal, or a chateau on the Seine. The concept of waterfront residence sparks our imaginations and allows our minds to dream of resplendence. Even Hollywood has etched and reinforced in film an indelible image of the glory of waterfront living.

The human desire for connection to the sea is as old as humanity itself; the longing to find ourselves seaside is innate and essential. We are drawn to the water, and for many people, living along the shore is both a fantasy and an aspiration. Constructing our own waterfront castle of dreams allows us to tap into visions of a life of sunning, sailing, and fishing – a life filled with joy and leisure.

Oceans, lakes, ponds, streams, or estuaries – what's your pleasure? Finding an ideal location for a dream home is the first challenge. There exists an increasing scarcity of available property along the water's edge because of environmental factors and governmental restrictions, which can make finding available un-built property in desirable areas a Herculean task.

Much of the prime waterfront property has been procured and homes built, and increasingly stringent state and federal regulatory standards restrict development along tidal and wetland areas. Navigating local building codes and zoning ordinances at times may seem daunting. Additionally, insurance carriers wary of liability for the damage wrought by repeated hurricanes in certain coastal regions are more selective about the types of properties they will protect. Com-plicating matters is the potential for insurance coverage for a house and its contents without comparable security for the land itself. In some beach areas, devastating storms have washed away not only landmark architecture but also the ground on which it stood.

The fulfillment of dreams seldom comes easily, but don't let that discourage you from dreaming. Today in more developed and desirable areas, undervalued buildings are either renovated or leveled to make room for the new.

Paging through this book, you will realize that finding a talented designer is the next step in the process of creating a waterfront home. Architects and builders assist people in transforming their dreams into reality. A good designer will first attempt to understand the way a client wishes to use the home, clarifying both pragmatic considerations such as types and numbers of rooms and more artistic matters related to reflecting the client's personality and way of life. The eventual plan unites these interests and translates them into form and space.

Great architects are limited only by the dreams and imaginations of their patrons. There is no "right" style for a waterfront home. The only style to consider is that which fits the client like a finely crafted garment. Some prefer contemporary designs while others lean toward the traditional, but many favor a blend of both. In the hands of a skilled designer, each can become a treasure.

The image of a fine waterfront home is based on an overall concept that drives its design. As the plans for the home progress, the architect and client frequently refer to the original concept to ensure its fit with the structure that is evolving. As the dream begins to take shape, new concepts will develop and unfold.

For a waterfront property, nautical themes are often interwoven into the image of the home, sometimes manifesting in subtle terms (e.g., a carefully

*Courtesy of © Anton Grassl Photography.*

detailed bracket or a marine cable rail) and other times becoming a prevalent part of the finished product (as in a house constructed to resemble a ship or a roof in the shape of a sail). Incorporating indigenous materials, regional building techniques, and local cultural artifacts may unite the building and the property on which it lies.

Regardless of the theme that motivates the design, a waterfront home must optimize the land upon which it is built. Siting should appraise such factors as solar orientation, topography, and desired views. For exposed waterfront sites, particularly in tidal areas, special attention must also be given to wind and wave patterns and their associated weather conditions. The unpredictable nature of these forces may influence not only the internal structure of the design but also the overall form and the selected building materials.

Cultural and philosophical factors may come into play as well. In the ancient Chinese art of Feng Shui, for example, wind and water are viewed as two of the most fundamental forms of life's energy. Consideration of the two will dictate both the siting of the house and the placement of the rooms within it.

Site opportunities and constraints and personal living and design preferences combine to inform both functionality of the plan and architectural style. Often, waterfront homes are designed so that the main living levels are located on the second floors and the bedrooms and other personal areas are situated on the ground floors. Although inverted from the design of most inland homes, this design offers the potential to gain greater and longer views in the unique setting that waterfront property affords. Of course, the reasons were quite different, but the notion of living on the second level actually dates back centuries to the waterfront city of Venice, where distinct site, function, and economic considerations mandated upper level residence.

Choosing a waterfront setting for your home often coincides with the yearning for a connection to the outdoors, so creating a design that reinforces strong interior and exterior relationships is often highly prized. Decks, terraces, balconies, and even outdoor showers help to unite the home with the property on

which it is situated. Physical connections and orientations of such amenities demand careful attention.

Decks, for example, are often a challenge when designing a home of traditional character. Decks came into fashion with the rise of 1950s post-war suburbia, which brought with it the demise of the street oriented front porch and a turn toward the privacy of backyard living. In general, a successful deck is designed in such a manner as to appear to be an integral part of the house rather than an appendage. Giving special attention to railing design as well as the features of the "skirt" (the area surrounding the house on the underside of the deck) is often vital to achieving this goal. Additionally, transitional spaces such as solariums and screened porches serve both indoor and outdoor functions and help to blur the boundaries between them.

Waterfront homes are a particularly interesting type of building because in most cases they have two fronts – there is no rear. Approach from land is generally by car and from the water typically by boat. Either direction must provide an inviting entrance to the home. Therefore, the entrances must also be distinct from one another, as each must respond to the unique characteristics of the landscape it faces.

Ultimately, navigating a balance between the opportunities and constraints of the site, the client's openness to ideas, and the architect's ability to listen and inspire will allow the creation of a successful design. In choosing to create a waterfront home, you are embarking on a magical voyage (see this next series of eight photos) and joining an elite group of visionaries who have anchored on the coastline throughout centuries. Pull up a rocking chair and relax, put your feet up on the railing, and enjoy the view!

—Clay Benjamin Smook AIA
smook@comcast.net
North Quincy, MA
January 2003

# Building a Waterfront House

## Across the Vineyard

The architectural vernacular for this house is deeply influenced by the works of Frank Lloyd Wright as well as Greene and Greene. Wright's Prairie style forms were marked by strong horizontal lines and low-hipped roofs. The Craftsman style homes of Greene and Greene offered inspiration on detailing.

In this photograph taken from the neighboring grape vineyard, the main house is on the left with garages and guest accommodations located in a separate building on the right. By juxtaposing the two structures, we formed a slate covered entry courtyard that acts as the initial entry experience to visitors. Guests are then lead into the solarium lush with exotic plants (a transitional indoor/outdoor space). Finally, the entry sequence culminates with entry into a north/south circulation spine that doubles as an art gallery and runs the full length of the house linking all main living spaces.

## The West Terrace

A life spent outdoors was one of the most important visions that the client had for the property. Unlike the Prairie homes whose exterior terraces were screened by high walls, this house is all about exterior space projecting outward, thrusting out to the water's edge.

The home is organized around three exterior terraces each with unique vistas and solar exposures. Pictured here is the west terrace, the main entertaining venue, which has a grand view of the water. To the far left is a screened porch, which is an extension of the dining room. In good weather, a glass wall between the two rooms disappears joining these two spaces into one.

The owner has a great love of showering outdoors year-round. At the second story is an outdoor shower off the master bathroom framed by a Craftsman style pergola – not yet constructed.

## Cantilevered Deck

The ten-foot cantilevered balcony off the master suite pays homage to Frank Lloyd Wright and his love of thrusting horizontal elements as a means of further tying the home into the landscape. Wright also countered and complemented his linear moves with a strong vertical mass. In this case, note the chimney constructed from indigenous stone. The siding, windows, and trim are all designed to reinforce the linear nature of the project.

## The Rocky Shores

The house sits perched over the water on a solid plinth of stone. Predominant views are directly to the north and west. These views informed the massing of the house. The house culminates subtly from the southern portion of the property northward. This approach to the disposition of volumes on the site maximizes views and limits the building from casting a shadow back on itself.

## Triangular Bay

A triangular bay projects from the breakfast area and reaches out to grasp the southeasterly morning sun. The stone wall of the east terrace is seen in the left portion of the photograph. By carving out these terraces, views were created from deep in the interior of the house, and light is allowed to penetrate far into the core. These courtyards serve as transitional spaces, framing views and protecting us from the elements.

The skin of the building is a combination of cedar shingles, clapboard, and vertical siding with custom-milled mahogany trim, all designed to reinforce the horizontal form of the building. The exquisite craftsmanship of this element, like so many others on the project, is a credit to the master carpenter on the site.

### The Tower

The engaged tower (under construction) punctuates the west terrace. Entrances to the art gallery/main circulation spine are to the right and left of the tower through French doors. Still yet to come are decorative brackets carved in the Craftsman style that will support the low shed roof.

On the second level is the owner's private office, which is on direct axis with one of his particularly favorite views of the sound.

### Family Room Interior

The interior of the family room begins to take shape. The room is marked by high coffered ceilings with custom-milled trim and casework and is punctuated by a stone fireplace with oversized hearth.

## Roofscape

The guest apartment was sited so that direct water views are maintained to the north and west past the main building. Looking diagonally northwest, however, the collage of hipped roofs of the main house break like waves against the skyline. A light monitor marks the pinnacle of the roof.

This central cupola element mirrors the traditional "widow's walk" found on homes in seafaring communities throughout New England. In this case, the cupola has operable windows and is located above the main grand stair. Flooding the core of the building with daylight, it also will allow passive cooling of the building: a chimney effect. When the French doors at the terraces are flung open, air will be drawn through the house upwards, creating a gentle breeze even on the hottest of summer days.

The roof cladding material is a "Green Product." Although it appears to be slate, it is, in fact, recycled automobile tires.

All above photos *Courtesy of Clay Benjamin Smook.*

Part One

# Castles

*Courtesy of D. Peter Lund.*

The private residence is built on a picturesque seaside site, offering a sweeping view of the Atlantic Ocean from both sides. *Courtesy of Mark C. Flannery, Photography.*

CBT/Childs Bertman Tseckares Inc. designed this residence on a one- and one-half acre waterfront site located within an established development. As a result, the design had to take into account pre-existing, moderately strict guidelines. Working through the conservation commission was one of the bigger challenges. *Courtesy of Mark C. Flannery, Photography.*

Far left:
The 6,500 square-foot structure is a traditional, Cape Cod shingle style home. The wraparound porch provides gracious views of the beach landscape and ocean while joining together all elements of the house. *Courtesy of ©Edward Jacoby.*

Left:
The many windows of the sitting room frame the outside views. *Courtesy of ©Edward Jacoby.*

Even the library integrates the outdoors.
*Courtesy of ©Edward Jacoby.*

The well-proportioned design, which skillfully masks the grand scale of the home, and the vernacular, Cape Cod exterior of indigenous materials create a complementary relationship between the residence and the landscape. *Courtesy of ©Edward Jacoby.*

CBT oriented the house to take advantage of the spectacular views and also to screen selected outdoor spaces from prevailing southwesterly winds. Designed to reflect the indigenous seaside resort architecture, it has an oversized roof, punched openings, and wide porches. *Courtesy of © Nick Wheeler.*

Designed as the summer home for a family of five, this house sits on a small, offshore island. A narrow causeway provides access to the island. The New England Regional Council and the American Institute of Architects gave CBT's design a Merit Award in 1991. The house is also known as "Island House" and "House on Buzzard's Bay." *Courtesy of D. Randolph Foulds Photography.*

The plan of the house is a cruciform with spaces, which radiate from a central mechanical core. Upon entrance to the house, steps lead down toward living areas, allowing for higher ceilings in areas of the house that see more activity. The higher ceilings also maximize views over the water. *Courtesy of © Nick Wheeler.*

The shape of the house reflects the simple pyramidal form of the plan. Each side of the pyramid varies slightly, reflecting the functional changes taking place within. *Courtesy of © Nick Wheeler.*

Over the center of the roof is a "widow's peak" tower, which affords 360-degree views and gives the house a traditional seaside appearance. This space is also the natural ventilator for the house, allowing through breezes. *Courtesy of © Nick Wheeler.*

The picturesque seaside site offers a sweeping 250-degree view of the Atlantic. *Courtesy of Mark C. Flannery, Photography.*

CBT's design for this year-round house provides a variety of opportunities to appreciate the peaceful environment. *Courtesy of Mark C. Flannery, Photography.*

The well proportioned design skillfully masks the grand scale of the home. *Courtesy of © Nick Wheeler.*

The design easily accommodates a large family as well as provides many gracious spaces – such as a dome – for entertaining. *Courtesy of © Nick Wheeler.*

*Left:*
There are numerous windows, balconies, a third-floor tower, and retreat. *Courtesy of © Nick Wheeler.*

*Right:*
The vernacular, Cape Cod exterior of indigenous materials creates a complementary relationship between the residence and the surrounding houses. *Courtesy of © Nick Wheeler.*

The relaxed design of this home complements its rustic resort location and respects the island's shingle style architecture. *Courtesy of Mark C. Flannery, Photography.*

Fully winterized for year-round use, the house is easily maintained and presents a variety of spaces for a family with young children. *Courtesy of ©Edward Jacoby.*

The design embraces the leisurely seaside styles of existing structures on the island. *Courtesy of ©Edward Jacoby.*

The great room permits both large parties and small intimate gatherings. *Courtesy of ©Edward Jacoby.*

People can flow easily in and out of the kitchen. *Courtesy of ©Edward Jacoby.*

CBT's sensitivity to island life inspired the application of indigenous forms and materials such as dormer windows, pitched roofs, articulated massing, cedar shingles, white trim, a red cedar roof, and large porches into the plan for this contemporary, 6,000 square-foot home. *Courtesy of ©Edward Jacoby.*

Arthur Cotton Moore FAIA designed a 4,000 square-foot house on a storm-thrashed, exposed point of land at the confluence of two major rivers. Corrosive saltwater spray is a severe problem in the area, and government setback restrictions allowed only a crooked sliver of a building pad – a little over one percent of the land. *Courtesy of Arthur Cotton Moore FAIA.*

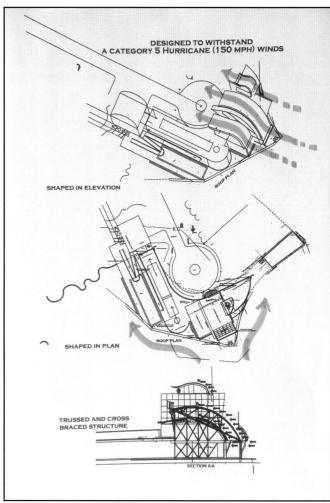

DESIGNED TO WITHSTAND
A CATEGORY 5 Hurricane (150 MPH) WINDS

SHAPED IN ELEVATION

ROOF PLAN

SHAPED IN PLAN

ROOF PLAN

TRUSSED AND CROSS
BRACED STRUCTURE

SECTION A-A

In an exposed waterfront location, the primary destructive force is the wind. This house is designed to withstand hurricane force winds by sloping and curving back in plan and elevation. Moore's design deflects the storm winds and expresses this basic windblown characteristic of coastal locations. *Courtesy of Arthur Cotton Moore FAIA.*

This view shows the sequence of roofs curving to address the wind. Because of the restricted site, Moore designed the roof as the principal terrace. It is pitched so it can also act as a major rain collector. *Courtesy of Arthur Cotton Moore FAIA.*

The interior of the living room displays the curved skylight with electronically operated shades. A series of sunshades – some mechanical, some fixed parts of the design – protect the house from solar gain. *Courtesy of Arthur Cotton Moore FAIA.*

This view from the master bedroom presents the curved channel sunshade and steel detailing of living room exterior beyond. Curved, rolled structural channels shade the bedroom wing and kitchen; the cantilevered portion of the ramp shades the rooms exposed to the western sun. *Courtesy of Arthur Cotton Moore FAIA.*

A spiral stair in the tower wall rises from the living room/library to the upper terrace and then to the top observation level. This view from the east shows the master bedroom and main steel wall supporting and giving access to the observation level. *Courtesy of Arthur Cotton Moore FAIA.*

Here, we see from the living room into kitchen beyond. The living room is a combination of two prototypes: the two-story balcony library and the glass conservatory. *Courtesy of Arthur Cotton Moore FAIA.*

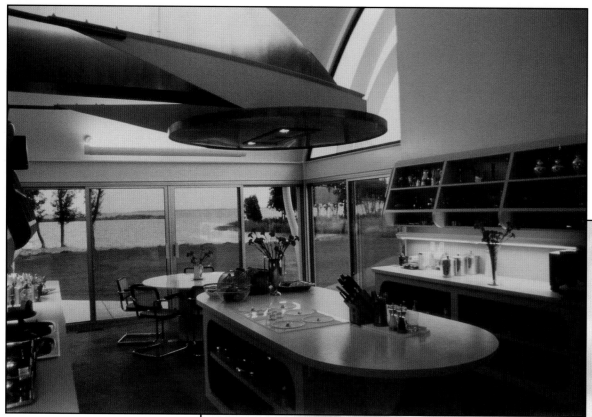

The shelves-only kitchen has a main work island serviced by a stainless steel hood, which recapitulates the shape of the room and adjacent porch. *Courtesy of Arthur Cotton Moore FAIA.*

This view from the south shows the circular porch, kitchen, living room, and master bedroom sections. *Courtesy of Arthur Cotton Moore FAIA.*

The west view shows the curved roofs and curved steel sunshades for the kitchen. On the exterior, minor elements like pole lights, entrance canopy, gutters, downspouts, and skylight servicing stair continue the windblown response. *Courtesy of Arthur Cotton Moore FAIA.*

The property has several fresh water ponds fed by six or seven springs. Each summer the Wampanogs lived around the ponds to obtain fresh water and fish and to access the ample shell food in the bay, only 200 yards away. Arrowheads and other artifacts are still found on the property. *Courtesy of D. Peter Lund.*

A minister, who came down from Harvard to Christianize the local Native Americans, built this house in 1742. He also built two adjacent houses for his sons in the 1780s. *Courtesy of D. Peter Lund.*

Arctic wild fowl, owls, Great Blue Herons, Ospreys, deer, and fox also visit the pond, which is a summer haven for Red Winged Blackbirds, Baltimore Orioles, Cedar Waxwings, and many other types of small birds. *Courtesy of D. Peter Lund.*

*Left:*
Today, the ponds are teeming with fish – the oddest of which are large (two feet long), colorful carp perhaps grown from "goldfish" someone dumped in the pond. The ponds also attract frogs, snakes, and turtles, including a very large, very old, female snapping turtle that walks around the property as if she owns it. *Courtesy of D. Peter Lund.*

The barn and its additions of the potting shed and the garage were built in three different centuries. *Courtesy of D. Peter Lund.*

The beautifully landscaped property has had only seven owners in 260 years. *Courtesy of D. Peter Lund.*

The current owners are the first ones to live here without a maid. *Courtesy of D. Peter Lund.*

The image is of the historic manor house as it appeared in 1989, prior to additions and renovations.
*Photo © Alan Karchmer.*

One of the primary goals of Muse Architects was to design all architectural and landscape work to be sympathetic with the historic manor house and to create a unified complex of buildings and gardens. This image shows the main house and the larger context of additions and renovations. The historic residence remains the most prominent structure on the property.
*Photo © Alan Karchmer.*

Set at the crest of the hill, the manor house offers panoramic views across the river.
*Photo © Alan Karchmer.*

The connection to the river is a significant feature of all the buildings. The pool house and terrace offer views to the river and shore. *Photo ©Alan Karchmer.*

Muse Architects designed the end wings and porches to be seamless and sympathetic to the historic manor house. *Photo © Alan Karchmer.*

From the porch, you can see the study with the renovated barns beyond. *Photo ©Alan Karchmer.*

As part of the renovation, this outbuilding, originally a garden shed, was converted into the owner's study with a sleeping loft above. *Photo ©Alan Karchmer.*

This kitchen, with all modern conveniences, is designed to complement the style of the existing manor house. *Photo ©Alan Karchmer.*

*Left:*
The sunroom addition to the main house allows for broad views to the river beyond. The exposed timber beams and stained wood trim are reminiscent of historic architecture of the area. *Photo ©Alan Karchmer.*

47

The additions made to this historic residence draw their inspiration from the original manor house and are sympathetic with the traditions of Maryland tidewater architecture. *Courtesy of Robert C. Lautman.*

From the exterior, the additions (kitchen/great room/porch/and master bedroom beyond) are divided into discrete forms, which are subordinate to the original manor house. *Courtesy of Robert C. Lautman.*

Together with the manor house additions, the pool house and terrace are complementary architectural elements within the landscape. *Courtesy of Robert C. Lautman.*

Muse Architects designed the swimming pool with a recessed edge towards the river, which allows for a seamless visual connection between the pool and the river beyond. *Courtesy of Robert C. Lautman.*

This image presents another view of the connection between the swimming pool and river. *Courtesy of Robert C. Lautman.*

The large glass pocket doors in the great room allow for the wall to open completely, connecting the room with the adjacent porch. *Courtesy of Robert C. Lautman.*

The master bedroom offers an intimate respite within the house. The large windows and glass door allow for an unobstructed river view. *Courtesy of Robert C. Lautman.*

Muse Architects chose to employ the footprint of the historic five part Maryland plan. The main body of this new weekend residence contains the areas that are regularly used while the northern and southern wings contain spaces that are used less often. *Courtesy of © Walter Smalling, Jr.*

The main body of the residence is projected onto the lawn, allowing a panoramic view of the waterfront. *Courtesy of © Walter Smalling, Jr.*

Twenty-six French doors along the facade allow for cross ventilation and easy access from the interior to the exterior. *Courtesy of © Walter Smalling, Jr.*

The conservatory is located adjacent to the living room, offering excellent views to the river. The space is detailed with floor-to-ceiling windows and a brick floor reminiscent of an enclosed porch. *Courtesy of © Walter Smalling, Jr.*

The main house uses a combination of brick paved and bleached oak floors. The walls are composed of pickled cedar and painted drywall. Windows offering river views surround the living spaces. *Courtesy of © Walter Smalling, Jr.*

From the master bedroom porch, the residents can observe the river beyond.
*Courtesy of © Walter Smalling, Jr.*

Muse Architects designed the pool house as a garden structure, recalling the details of the main house. It also provides private guest quarters. *Photo ©Alan Karchmer.*

The pool house includes a large living room, a bathroom/changing room, and a kitchen. The walls are painted drywall, and the ceiling is pickled cedar with a large central skylight. Flagstone is used for the interior flooring and the exterior terrace beyond the French doors. *Photo ©Alan Karchmer.*

Muse Architects designed a 6,000 square-foot residence on a waterfront site. Because of regulatory concerns, the design elevated the main living area to the second floor, with bedrooms on the third floor. *Photo ©Alan Karchmer.*

A dramatic roofline as well as the use of white painted clapboard against bleached wood shingles minimizes the height of the three-story structure. The bleached wood shingles also help the house to blend with its wooded site. *Photo ©Alan Karchmer.*

The waterfront facade incorporates exterior terraces and porches, allowing the interior rooms to open towards the water. *Photo © Alan Karchmer.*

The living room porch looks towards the river. *Photo © Alan Karchmer.*

The living room faces the river and opens to the waterfront porches on either side.
*Photo © Alan Karchmer.*

The dining room doubles as a library, displaying a collection of books.
*Photo © Alan Karchmer.*

The dramatic central stair is crowned by a large skylight, which permits natural light to filter down through the various floors. The stairwell walls are clad with a combination of board and batten and open slatted wood. *Photo © Alan Karchmer.*

*Right:*
The elegance of paradise under the stars is evident in this house built by DiPrima Fine Homes. *Courtesy of DiPrima Fine Homes.*

*Far right:*
The 4,700 square-foot Villa Viscaya is waterfront living in a stunning setting. *Courtesy of DiPrima Fine Homes.*

Experience the luxury…a lush tropical landscape in your own backyard. *Courtesy of DiPrima Fine Homes.*

Even flossing is wonderful in this flower-adorned bathroom. *Courtesy of DiPrima Fine Homes.*

Breakfast in bed is a must in this bright bedroom.
*Courtesy of DiPrima Fine Homes.*

Dining is an event in this house.
*Courtesy of DiPrima Fine Homes.*

The large living room is divided into different seating areas. *Courtesy of DiPrima Fine Homes.*

Located on a bulb-shaped peninsula, this project is the result of a phased design plan developed by Clay Benjamin Smook AIA for the property. The complexity of the programmatic site and regulatory considerations, coupled with a limited initial budget, demanded that the project be designed and executed over time. *Courtesy of © Anton Grassl Photography.*

The initial phase began with the construction of a simple, yet elegant, two-story structure in the middle of a scenic saltwater pond. Subsequently, Smook designed a series of complementary forms using the original gabled form as the framework. *Courtesy of Alex S. MacLean.*

The house is clad in a traditional palette of wood siding composed in an unusual manner. The white cedar shingles are configured in alternating courses of five-inch and two-inch exposures, forming a solid "rusticated base" to the building. This is juxtaposed with the red cedar clapboard siding that marks the body of the house. *Courtesy of © Anton Grassl Photography.*

The layout of the house is a "flip flop" design with the main living levels located on the second floor to attain the long water views, as well as views back to the building itself. *Courtesy of © Anton Grassl Photography.*

*Left:*
With main living on the top level, guests are led from the entry foyer up a dramatic stair accented with form and flooded with light. The path to the second floor gently winds its way up and around a "crows' nest," which serves as a promontory for stargazing. *Courtesy of © Anton Grassl Photography.*

*Bottom left:*
The entry piazza is defined by a glass block enclosed outdoor cabana, with master suite above (to the left) and the garage with screened porch (to the right). *Courtesy of © Anton Grassl Photography.*

*Below:*
The island paradise rises above the fog. *Courtesy of ©Anton Grassl Photography.*

**Opposing page:**

*Far left:*
Weber Murphy Fox designed a major addition to an existing 6,000 square-foot residence. The design added 7,000 square feet with new master bedroom, great room, and an indoor swimming pool complex. The firm also renovated the residence to enlarge the formal dining room, enlarge the kitchen, and provide a new terrace. The image presents the new dining room bay as seen through the terrace portico. *Courtesy of Art Becker.*

*Top right:*
The new great room addition (right) frames the new flagstone terrace. An outdoor swimming pool, a hot tub, fountain, and a fire pit grace the terrace. The firm designed the trellis, trim, and details to harmonize with and reflect the existing bay edge gazebo and residence. *Courtesy of Art Becker.*

*Bottom right:*
The piano is the focal point of the new great room. *Courtesy of Art Becker.*

The design added two semi-round bays to the house, one as the dining room extension and one as the north extension to the great room. The round north bay provides intimate lake viewing and a stage for string quartets. *Courtesy of Art Becker.*

The new design expanded the existing gazebo into a cliff overhang deck. *Courtesy of Art Becker.*

The new great room addition (right) frames the terrace at night. *Courtesy of Art Becker.*

The axial fountain reinforces the formal entrance. *Courtesy of Art Becker*.

Weber Murphy Fox configured the new great room to display a large art collection, to entertain large gatherings, and to be used by the family. *Courtesy of Art Becker*.

The design remodeled and expanded the kitchen. *Courtesy of Art Becker.*

Design soothes the soul. The master bath for this spectacular house designed by Siemasko + Verbridge (see front cover) offers dramatic ocean views from the freestanding, oval bathtub. The space features a fireplace, dressing table, and double sinks. Toilet room and a steam shower are separate. *Courtesy of Robert Benson.*

The master bedroom offers breathtaking ocean views from the curved windows. It features a gabled domed ceiling lit by sconces, a fireplace, and a custom headboard. *Courtesy of Robert Benson.*

The master closet has a coffee maker, sink, and refrigerator. The custom cabinetry is accented with Italian light fixtures. *Courtesy of Robert Benson.*

The main house is constructed on the site of the original 1900 manor house. Sited high above sea level, it features beautifully landscaped grounds with lawns sloping seaward and dramatic ocean views. *Courtesy of Siemasko + Verbridge.*

Constructed of stone and shingles, its presence anchors the property in a manner reminiscent of turn-of-the-century estates. *Courtesy of Robert Benson.*

The *porte cochere* offers a glimpse of the exquisite attention to detail to be found throughout the home. The image is of the ceiling. *Courtesy of Robert Benson.*

The formal entry opens into an octagonal great hall. Directly across are Doric columns separating the great hall from the dining room with ocean views beyond. *Courtesy of Robert Benson.*

The coatroom has leather paneled walls and floor, with a cobalt blue chandelier. *Courtesy of Robert Benson.*

*Left:*
The kitchen has mahogany cabinets with glass panels, sandblasted glass backsplashes, and stone countertops. Note the dual sinks (one for him and one for her or maybe one for dishes and one for pots) and the bar sink. *Courtesy of Robert Benson.*

*Below:*
The family room is boat shaped with mahogany paneled walls, mahogany cabinetry, fireplace, thin screen television, and one wall of glass facing onto the terrace with ocean views beyond. *Courtesy of Robert Benson.*

A mahogany paneled study with a fireplace and window alcove offers a wet bar and glimpses of the ocean. *Courtesy of Robert Benson.*

The pool house kitchen has an oven, dishwasher, and refrigerator. *Courtesy of Avanti Studios.*

*Left:*
The pool house retains the footprint of the former 1960s pool house. Tucked into the wooded portion of the property, it creates a juxtaposition of woodland and contemporary ease. *Courtesy of Avanti Studios.*

The formal and informal gardens have utilized the remains of the old gardens, including the game lawn, orchard, and wildflower field leading to the beach access. *Courtesy of Siemasko + Verbridge.*

*Left:*
Overlooking the water, this residence designed by Interdesign Limited has weathered, white, Canadian cedar shingle walls and a hand split cedar roof. The custom, large paned windows frame the ocean view. The hurricane sliding shutters built into the construction as well as the functioning, wood, hurricane, swinging shutter panels comply with insurance regulations. *Courtesy of Woodruff/Brown Photography.*

The living room has pickled ash paneling and floors. The screen porch at the end of the room has a commanding view of the water, as does the box bay window at the left. *Courtesy of Woodruff/Brown Photography.*

The kitchen/breakfast area has custom ash cabinets and granite countertops. The appliance garage/island screens the working space from the great room. *Courtesy of Woodruff/Brown Photography.*

The foyer has views through the screen porch to the ocean. The custom mahogany door and handrail system is especially designed for the four-story residence. *Courtesy of Woodruff/Brown Photography.*

The entrance auto courtyard and exterior stair system up to the main-floor level accommodate flood plain zone regulations. The garage on the left has a roof designed to subordinate the garage doors and place them in shadow. The screen porch overlooks the water. *Courtesy of Woodruff/Brown Photography.*

The greenhouse foyer of this house designed by Interdesign Limited has a fieldstone floor. To disperse drainage from watering plants, no grout was used. In the distance are windows overlooking the Mystic Seaport and the famous ship, the "Charles Morgan." The compass rose is of bird's-eye maple and rosewood inlaid into the teak floor. *Courtesy of © Karen Bussolini.*

This view is from the inner foyer to outer foyer with the custom African mahogany door and custom transom glass. Glass roof and walls form the atrium entry. *Courtesy of © Karen Bussolini.*

The dining room overlooks the harbor and the "Charles Morgan." It has custom paneling and a contemporary style glass handrail with mahogany wood carved to resemble ship's rope with gold whipping at the end. *Courtesy of © Karen Bussolini.*

The kitchen/family eating area has a seating group at the French doors facing the water. To bring the south sun into the space, the firm created a barrel vaulted ceiling as well as fan light windows on either side of the fireplace. The dual televisions with headsets on either side of the fireplace keep peace among the children. *Courtesy of © Karen Bussolini.*

This house designed by Interdesign Limited has a view to the river, the sound, and carp pool below. A waterfall from the terrace level spills onto native rocks carved to form containment pools for aquatic plants. At left is the living room/screen porch pavilion, where twenty-one feet of glass slide into architectural pockets, creating an indoor/outdoor environment. Across the pool is the second of three structures housing three levels. The guest bedroom is seen below main floor and dining area. On the third level on the other side of the pyramid is a spectacular bedroom suite with a commanding view. *Courtesy of © 89 Durston Saylor.*

Foyer is in foreground with partial view of the living room/screen porch pavilion. Floors in both these spaces are French limestone squares with a bluestone border; the wood details are red and white cedar. The exterior walls are of native stone. *Courtesy of ©89 Durston Saylor.*

Living room central seating area and bluestone bench seat at windows provide abundant short-term seating and overlooks the pools and river. The architect selected the antique carpet because of the color and the pattern, which complement the breathtaking outdoor views. *Courtesy of ©89 Durston Saylor.*

The fireplace is a square, opening catty-corner in the room. The ceiling soars to twenty-seven feet. A soffit conceals uplighting as well as pin spots to highlight artwork and sculpture. The ceiling is made from red cedar planks overlapped to show their thickness as well as to create texture. The white cedar walls are in random widths, and the floor is French limestone squares with a bluestone border. *Courtesy of ©89 Durston Saylor.*

The see-through fireplace is situated in the kitchen, dining, breakfast, and family spaces. Native stone is used as the floating slab hearth and firebox. Fireplace surround is stucco. Floors are random width, curly maple. *Courtesy of ©89 Durston Saylor.*

The dining area has a birds-eye maple table and classic Hans Wagner teak dining chairs. A camel hair runner is used as a foil with nature. Wall sculpture and small paintings are hung on the exterior walls so as not to compete with nature seen through the large glass expanses. *Courtesy of ©89 Durston Saylor.*

The breakfast bay/skylight has views to the water. Dining room table is seen in foreground; to the left is the island with double ovens acting as a pedestal and concealing the working kitchen area. *Courtesy of ©89 Durston Saylor.*

The sofa at left is built into the main kitchen island. The see-through fireplace brings warmth to the room. In the distance is the dining area, which is large enough to seat ten people in comfort. *Courtesy of ©89 Durston Saylor.*

Kitchen seating sofa has Tory style deck beyond. Pennsylvania bluestone counters tie in with the native stone. The curly maple cabinets and khaki color walls soften the brightness. *Courtesy of ©89 Durston Saylor.*

The hub of the house, the kitchen, is a wonderful gathering place. The custom, four-foot bronze sink is often filled with white wine bottles, for a wine tasting evening for sixty to eighty people. The eighteen-foot main island with appliance garage, double ovens, and built-in sofa is in the background. *Courtesy of ©89 Durston Saylor.*

Master bath sink counter is bluestone with custom pottery sink mounted on top. White cedar walls, maple floor, and French limestone shower basin complete the room. The shower affords exceptional views. *Courtesy of ©89 Durston Saylor.*

The third-floor master suite has a deck recessed into the pyramid roof with a tray ceiling. Wraparound windows look to the water. Master bath is through the double door. *Courtesy of ©89 Durston Saylor.*

The walk surface is bluestone with Mexican black beach rocks complementing whale-like boulders. On right is the fieldstone living pavilion. At left is the larger pyramid with kitchen, dining, and family spaces. *Courtesy of ©89 Durston Saylor.*

The Tory gate deck off the kitchen has a view of the water. Bench seats and the two-foot band with a low rail on top form a barrier to protect people from falling into the native laurel twenty feet below. Deck surface is red cedar laid on edge to form a pleasant walking surface. *Courtesy of ©89 Durston Saylor.*

# Part Two

# C o t t a g e s

*Courtesy of D. Peter Lund.*

*Courtesy of D. Peter Lund.*

*Courtesy of D. Peter Lund.*

*Courtesy of D. Peter Lund.*

Trees are for climbing, flowers for picking, and water for swimming in this riverfront home. To reach the house, you drive through a sunny meadow. *Courtesy of D. Peter Lund.*

You pass through ripe gardens, where the delphinium sends up long purple spikes. *Courtesy of D. Peter Lund.*

A tree shaded porch surrounds two sides of the house. *Courtesy of D. Peter Lund.*

Across the river stands the rock cliff where, according to local storytellers, a Native American chief would sit to watch his enemies' canoes approach. Some add that he pushed any unfaithful maidens in the tribe over the cliff. *Courtesy of D. Peter Lund.*

It is the river, however, that dominates. *Courtesy of D. Peter Lund.*

Despite the legends, you find serenity on this porch. *Courtesy of D. Peter Lund.*

Views of the river dominate the great room. *Courtesy of D. Peter Lund.*

A wicker lounge allows you to relax with the calico cat and put the rest of world on hold. *Courtesy of D. Peter Lund.*

The upstairs bedrooms retain a simple pine look. *Courtesy of D. Peter Lund.*

This peaceful retreat overlooks the marshes at the end of the country road. *Courtesy of D. Peter Lund.*

Water has long been a source of inspiration for artists, writers, and those of us who like to muse about life and the way it is. *Courtesy of D. Peter Lund.*

Externally, this house appears to be a modest rectangle. *Courtesy of D. Peter Lund.*

It is the marshes that you notice. *Courtesy of D. Peter Lund.*

Inside, the house seems to be much larger than its simple and unimposing facade. *Courtesy of D. Peter Lund.*

The pond mirrors the sky and the trees surrounding this cottage. *Courtesy of D. Peter Lund.*

The wood stove is for those days when the mists seep and wind their way around the land. *Courtesy of D. Peter Lund.*

A quiet lunch awaits guests. *Courtesy of D. Peter Lund.*

The kitchen keeps a silent watch on the pond and its wildlife. *Courtesy of D. Peter Lund.*

Local antique shops help to furnish the cottage. *Courtesy of D. Peter Lund.*

Externally, the house is much simpler than it appears from the interior.
*Courtesy of D. Peter Lund.*

A junkyard treasure hovers in front of the view.
*Courtesy of D. Peter Lund.*

This house on a tidal estuary pays homage to the Shingle and Arts and Crafts styles of the late nineteenth and early twentieth centuries often found in New England summer communities. *Courtesy of Don Ritz, Architect.*

Don Ritz, Architect, designed the living area so it would incorporate sweeping views of conservation land across a tidal estuary. *Courtesy of R.W. Green.*

The interior has a contemporary appearance with its continuous flow of space, while the details are traditional in the form of classical columns, thin spindle stair rails, and natural wood kitchen cabinets. *Courtesy of R.W. Green.*

Some of the hallmarks of the Shingle style here are "eyebrow" dormers, a continuous surface of natural shingles without corner boards, and classical columns both inside and out. Arts and Crafts style elements include exposed rafter tails, a porch low to the ground, and hip roofs. *Courtesy of Don Ritz, Architect.*

The continuous cornice unifies the cabinets.
*Courtesy of R.W. Green.*

The second-floor bedroom has water views
from its corner window. *Courtesy of R.W. Green.*

The master bedroom features an eyebrow dormer opening into a vaulted ceiling with the patio door to the balcony below. *Courtesy of R.W. Green.*

The porch offers wonderful water views. *Courtesy of Don Ritz, Architect.*

Don Ritz designed this second-floor addition to a simple bungalow to take advantage of sweeping water views. Jeanne Baravella is responsible for interior and landscape design. *Courtesy of Don Ritz, Architect.*

The wood stove and TV alcove cabinet make this a popular gathering place. *Courtesy of R.W. Green.*

Water views can be had – even through the
bathroom shower. *Courtesy of R.W. Green.*

The second-floor addition contributes a dramatically high
ceiling and transom windows. *Courtesy of R.W. Green.*

The addition provided exterior living space through a roof deck accessed via a hatch and folding stairs. A ground-level terrace offers sweeping views of a nature preserve across a salt marsh and estuary. *Courtesy of R.W. Green.*

The original, ranch type house had insufficient windows and did not fit in with its more traditional neighbors. Ritz designed an addition consisting of an upper-level master bedroom suite and a first-floor sunroom, both with bands of windows, to enjoy the panoramic view. *Courtesy of R.W. Green.*

*Right:*
The two-level deck with pyramidal pergola allows enjoyment of the water views. *Courtesy of Don Ritz, Architect.*

*Far right:*
Stepped windows and traditional details combine old and new in this waterfront home. *Courtesy of Don Ritz, Architect.*

**Opposing page:**

*Top left:*
The traditional hipped pergola is detailed in the classical manner. *Courtesy of Don Ritz, Architect.*

*Bottom left:*
The two-level deck, along with the pergola, form a light and airy tower, allowing views through from the interior. *Courtesy of Don Ritz, Architect.*

*Top right:*
The first-floor family room has bead board wainscot and patio doors to the lower deck. *Courtesy of Don Ritz, Architect.*

*Bottom right:*
The master bedroom has a view of the lighthouse. *Courtesy of R.W. Green.*

Situated on a rocky beachfront, this small house features a bold, angled, turret dormer with hipped roof designed by Don Ritz, Architect. The late 1800s Shingle style provides the inspiration for the simple yet playful free forms of dormers, hipped gables, turrets, and bays that made the style so popular for the summer resort cottages of New England. *Courtesy of Don Ritz, Architect.*

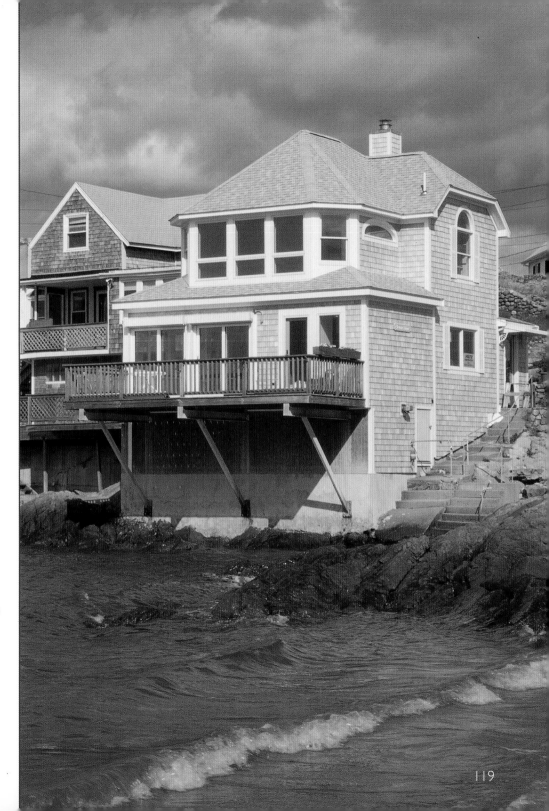

In the late 1800s, a prominent Boston architect designed a wraparound porch for this seaside resort house. A few tantalizing photos of the decayed porch just prior to its demolition along with some fragments of the original components provided Ritz with enough information to recreate the original porch. *Courtesy of Don Ritz, Architect.*

Concrete steps leading directly to the beach blend in with the geology and make the beach a usable extension to the house – at least at low tide. The deck, cantilevered on steel brackets, provides outside living space when high water covers the beach. *Courtesy of Don Ritz, Architect.*

The Victorian bracket, post, and rail details complete the historically accurate design. *Courtesy of Don Ritz, Architect.*

The hipped roof pavilion accentuates the corner and forms an outdoor room to enjoy the water views. *Courtesy of Don Ritz, Architect.*

This 800 square-foot, west facing guest residence shares its lakeside site with the owner's 5,000 square-foot main house. Designed by Thielsen Architects, Inc., and built in 2000 by Moss Bay Homes, the cottage shares a common wall with a neighbor's guesthouse. The sweeping overhangs protect the window wall from the winter rains. *Photo by Steve Keating.*

The entry stairs and walk meander through a lavishly landscaped garden and past the guest bedroom before approaching the entry. *Photo by Steve Keating.*

Through the use of an expansive window wall and double height ceilings, the living space appears much larger than its actual area. The open loft that floats over the kitchen/dining space provides a sense of shelter. *Photo by Steve Keating.*

The spiral stair from the main floor to the loft offers a panoramic view of the lake and the downtown skyline. The open loft doubles as the master suite and home office. *Photo by Steve Keating.*

Viewed from the loft, the lowered ceiling of the lineal entry creates a subtle transition from the cottage exterior to the warmth and intimacy of the interior as it opens into the two-story living space. Changes in wall color accentuate this transition. *Photo by Steve Keating.*

The redwood sided house overlooks the water. *Courtesy of Stephen Cridland.*

This house designed by Zaik/Miller Associates is located in a historic beach village, on a gentle, sloping, southerly property overlooking the river, bay, and ocean. *Courtesy of Stephen Cridland.*

The central space is a gracious, two-story living area, including kitchen and dining area. *Courtesy of Stephen Cridland.*

The site for this Zaik/Miller home is a rocky knoll overlooking one of the finest, wild trout fishing streams in the United States. *Courtesy of Zaik/Miller Associates.*

Light flows through this lovely cottage. *Courtesy of Zaik/Miller Associates.*

A strong, two-story "spine" accesses well organized spaces and elegant materials. *Courtesy of Zaik/Miller Associates.*

*Right:*
The house is "wedded" to this site, maximizing a southerly orientation for view. *Courtesy of Zaik/Miller Associates.*

Christine Albertsson designed this lakeside retreat when she was with MS&R (Minneapolis, Minnesota). She retained the original outdoor fireplace, which was the inspiration for the stone work in the project. © Peter Bastianelli-Kerze.

A four season porch with stone floors and small fireplace leads out to a terrace overlooking the lake. © Peter Bastianelli-Kerze.

The great room has an open kitchen and rough-hewn timber trusses, which compliment the fieldstone fireplace. © Peter Bastianelli-Kerze.

A covered, open log work carport connects the bunkhouse to the cabin. The kitchen windows overlook the enclosed yard. © *Peter Bastianelli-Kerze.*

The house and garage, designed by MS&R, Ltd., with Christine Albertsson, enclose a circular drive. A four season porch overlooks the lake. © *Peter Bastianelli-Kerze.*

*Right:*
The porch was built to replicate the original, but the ceilings were raised to give an airier feel. © *Peter Bastianelli-Kerze.*

132

The open interior features a built-in bench at the dining area and a raised counter with seating, which is open to the kitchen. © *Peter Bastianelli-Kerze.*

# Part Three

# Communities

*Courtesy of D. Peter Lund.*

*Courtesy of D. Peter Lund.*

Beautiful Oregon Southshore Oceanfront Condominiums are constructed from concrete, which gives them increased structural safety – an important feature when you live on the Oregon coast with its fierce winter storms. *Courtesy of Terry Poe Photography.*

The great room of this beautiful 2,520 square-foot condominium is perfect for entertaining guests and allows spectacular views of the Pacific – even from the granite breakfast bar. *Courtesy of Terry Poe Photography.*

The condos range from two bedroom, two bath to three bedroom, three bath homes. *Courtesy of Terry Poe Photography*.

The units range in size from 1,375 to 2,520 square-feet. All have built-in features like central wiring systems for phone, cable TV, security, speakers, computers, intercoms, extra electrical plugs, and even Christmas lighting on request. *Courtesy of Terry Poe Photography*.

Pour in those bath salts, light some candles and enjoy a nice sunset from the Jacuzzi tub, which separates master bath and bedroom. *Courtesy of Terry Poe Photography.*

The extensive use of glass allows a nearly unobstructed view of the Pacific. By using Formtech™ Insulated Concrete walls, Oregon South Shore Contractors can add 25% more glass. *Courtesy of Terry Poe Photography.*

Little Whale Cove is a small development designed by Zaik/Miller on a rocky stretch of the Oregon coast. These houses are situated in steeply sloped, spruce tree forests. *Courtesy of Zaik/Miller Associates.*

The houses are designed with adequate overhangs, shingled roofs and walls, and grand vistas. *Courtesy of Zaik/Miller Associates.*

The development overlooks the ocean with all its mystery. *Courtesy of Zaik/Miller Associates.*

Quechee Lakes has 5,200 acres of Vermont countryside and two private championship golf courses designed by Geoffrey Cornish. The Highland Course plays just over 6,765 yards from the back tees and features a combination of gently rolling and elevated tree lined fairways, and rock wall bunkers. *Courtesy of Quechee Lakes Development Company.*

The Lakeland Course measures approximately 6,570 yards from the back tees, and presents more of a links style design that incorporates trees, bunkers, and water features. The impressive layouts and dramatic finishing holes of the Quechee Lakes golf courses have earned accolades from both *Golf Digest* and *Vermont Golf* magazines. *Courtesy of Quechee Lakes Development Company.*

Bold Adirondack design and two expansive decks off the master suite and living room are highlights of the Windsor, a 2,978 square-foot home. *Courtesy of Quechee Lakes Development Company.*

The Newbury, a contemporary Vermont farmhouse with 2,650 square-feet offers an abundance of natural light and high-end finishing touches. The Newbury's large windows provide woodland, valley, and river views. *Courtesy of Quechee Lakes Development Company.*

The bedroom looks out on the lovely Vermont countryside. *Courtesy of Quechee Lakes Development Company.*

Part Four

# Cliffhangers

*Courtesy of D. Peter Lund.*

Courtesy of D. Peter Lund.

Courtesy of D. Peter Lund.

*Courtesy of D. Peter Lund.*

The house looks like a Cape from the driveway.
*Courtesy of D. Peter Lund.*

149

But it is much larger than a Cape.
*Courtesy of D. Peter Lund.*

The paneled library looks out on the water.
*Courtesy of D. Peter Lund.*

As do the living room, the kitchen, and other rooms. *Courtesy of D. Peter Lund.*

The master bath also has a dramatic water view. There you can leave the world behind and just savor the beauty. *Courtesy of D. Peter Lund.*

Imagine living with a view like this. *Courtesy of D. Peter Lund.*

The pool overlooks the cove.
*Courtesy of D. Peter Lund.*

Often, you can see bald eagles soaring over the water. They plummet down and use their talons to grab the fish without touching the water. In the winter, when an eagle catches a large fish, it may eat the fish on the ice, surrounded by anxious crows and gulls waiting for tidbits. *Courtesy of D. Peter Lund.*

When you walk down the dirt road, you hear the occasional splash of a fish jumping in the quarry ponds, the birds fluttering in their nests, and the drip of last night's rain falling from the forest roof. Then, you come to the house standing in the middle of the forest. *Courtesy of D. Peter Lund.*

The main room houses kitchen, dining, and living areas. *Courtesy of D. Peter Lund.*

The master bedroom and bath are the entire second floor. Any guests sleep in a separate two room guesthouse. *Courtesy of D. Peter Lund.*

When you sit on the terrace, you look down, down, down. *Courtesy of D. Peter Lund*

This contemporary cliffhanger is nestled just above the river. *Courtesy of D. Peter Lund.*

The freewheeling spatial pattern allows everyone to enjoy the water views. *Courtesy of D. Peter Lund.*

The owner of this home had dreams and a plan. He kept searching until he found a ledge overlooking the water. An architect helped him rework the plans and pin the house to the ledge. *Courtesy of D. Peter Lund.*

Cooling devices are rarely needed with the cross draft and the river breezes. *Courtesy of D. Peter Lund.*

Of course, there is a fireplace. *Courtesy of D. Peter Lund.*

The house is wholly integrated with its setting. The cliffs are part of the bedroom. *Courtesy of D. Peter Lund.*

Light and stone surround the master bathroom. *Courtesy of D. Peter Lund.*

The driveway is a long curve to the top of the cliff. *Courtesy of D. Peter Lund.*

The high bluff overlooking the sound was special. The new owner just needed to construct a more contemporary house using the existing footprint. *Courtesy of D. Peter Lund.*

Into his new house, the owner built terraces with spacious views. *Courtesy of D. Peter Lund.*

The Juliet balconies permit the owner to watch the boats in the channel. Note that the balconies are made secure by a thin metal rope, which doesn't interfere with the view. *Courtesy of D. Peter Lund.*

The design of the house creates a casual feeling. *Courtesy of D. Peter Lund.*

The cook likes the panorama too. *Courtesy of D. Peter Lund.*

Even the pianist can see the waves curling in the distance. *Courtesy of D. Peter Lund.*

The color of the lavatory basin mirrors that of the sea. *Courtesy of D. Peter Lund.*

Sitting here on a summer day listening to the murmur of the ocean or watching the clouds float across the sky is hardly a waste of time. *Courtesy of D. Peter Lund.*

This charming 2,700 square-foot house designed by Eric Brandt, Architect, is perched on a 150 foot cliff overlooking Oak Creek Valley, Cathedral Rock, and Sedona. Just 150 feet below the patio, Oak Creek twists, turns and tumbles over rocks. *Courtesy of Allan Briney.*

The renovation honored the strong shell of the original adobe brick home. It did, however, gut the original 1968 interior, raise the ceilings, and create a fabulous one-bedroom home. The only floor area added is the new media room within a former one-car garage. The view from here is from the gate to the patio. *Courtesy of Allan Briney.*

In the kitchen, copper accents include a hammered copper counter and splash. The main countertops are Silestone. The cabinets are a mix of maple with a natural finish and grooved panels painted green. *Courtesy of Allan Briney.*

The kitchen overlooks the living room and the dramatic view beyond. The new raised ceilings with exposed structural beams offer airiness and drama. *Courtesy of Allan Briney.*

The owner, a ceramist, created the fireplace tiles. The coyote on the hearth is also her work. *Courtesy of Allan Briney.*

Imagine waking up every morning with this view from the master bedroom. A private pool and spa are adjacent to the master suite. *Courtesy of Allan Briney.*

This image is the front entry (west side) of the house. The guest quarters, ceramic workshop and kiln, and a three car garage are in a separate, new ranch style building. *Courtesy of Allan Briney.*

A central courtyard has a new koi pond with another red rock fountain. The courtyard's original concrete paving was stained and grouted to resemble tiles. *Courtesy of Allan Briney.*

The koi are always moving. *Courtesy of Allan Briney.*

Through the office windows, you see the koi patio and Cathedral Rock in the distance. *Courtesy of Allan Briney.*

This residence, designed by Robert Oshatz, Architect, appears to be floating in space. The site is a 23,000 square-foot lot, sloping up from the street. The house is a three-story structure with each story being a split-level for a total of six levels. *Courtesy of Steve Allen.*

The driveway leads to a carport and entry situated in the middle level. Spanning the carport is a sitting and master bedroom suite. To the right of the carport is a split-level entry that leads up to the living room and balcony above the funnel shape form. Beyond the funnel shape, you can see the river. *Courtesy of Robert Oshatz, Architect.*

Standing by a stone planter circle, you can follow a pathway and steps down to the studio entry and deck. The funnel-shape bedroom is well defined with the living room balcony above. *Courtesy of Steve Allen.*

This view is taken from the carport, looking toward the entry door. To the left is the copper clad, mushroom shape kitchen above one funnel-shape bedroom. To the right is the living room balcony above the other funnel-shape bedroom. *Courtesy of Robert Oshatz, Architect.*

The three-story structure cantilevers out of the hillside. The lower level has a teen room and studio space with its own entrance. The children's bedrooms are in the middle level; the family community spaces and master bedroom suite are on the upper level. The cantilever upper level is a dining room balcony. The copper and glazed mushroom shape houses the kitchen. *Courtesy of Robert Oshatz, Architect.*

*Right:*
The living/dining area has the warm glow of natural wood. An entertainment area with audio/video equipment, sofa/day bed, and built-in desk is on the split-level up from the living area. *Courtesy of Steve Allen.*

Oshatz's design draws the eye out to focus on the river and mountain beyond. Notice how the materials inside proceed through the glazing and continue outward. *Courtesy of Steve Allen.*

The spectacular river view proceeds beyond the cabinet that separates the kitchen from the living/dining area. *Courtesy of Robert Oshatz, Architect.*

*Right:*
The dining area has custom beveled cedar walls. *Courtesy of Steve Allen.*

**Opposing page:**

*Far left:*
In this view from the dining deck, you can see the fin wall. Continuing out from the house, it deflects the strong river winds and reduces the noise from the road behind the house. *Courtesy of Robert Oshatz, Architect.*

*Top right:*
The kitchen, semi-circular in plan and section, provides a panoramic view from the window seat. This space is a combination kitchen/family area featuring a built-in table and large granite counter areas. *Courtesy of Steve Allen.*

*Bottom right:*
The sliding sandblasted glass doors separate the sitting room from the master bedroom suite. When these doors slide back to create one large space, you can lie in bed and see through the living/dining area to marvel at the view beyond. *Courtesy of Steve Allen.*

This family home is perched forty-five feet above the beach on a steep, heavily vegetated hillside. Zaik/Miller designed and constructed the house to harmonize with the natural vegetation and deal with strong wind and extreme weather. *Courtesy of Zaik/Miller Associates.*

A circular staircase leads to a loft lookout area. The children's bedrooms are on different levels to maintain privacy. *Courtesy of Zaik/Miller Associates.*

There's nothing like a sunset. *Courtesy of Zaik/Miller Associates.*

A carp pool surrounds this Balinese style house designed by Interdesign Limited. It sits on a 160-foot cliff overlooking the harbor and the river. Sliding windows overlooking the pool and waterfall open into architectural pockets, leaving no glass to obstruct the view and the sounds of nature. The stone path in the pool connects the dining room to living room terrace. *Courtesy of Woodruff/Brown Photography.*

The living room corner has steps in the distance up to the dining room/kitchen wing. The master bedroom is on the upper level with a deck carved into the roof. Copper clad roof caps and hip corners and a five shingle, cedar starter course at the roof edge contribute to the unique architectural features. *Courtesy of Woodruff/Brown Photography.*

The design called for elephant gray stucco walls, natural stone, and a cedar roof so the house would blend in with the rock cliffs and surrounding nature conservancy land. The guest house and moon gate are on the left. *Courtesy of Woodruff/Brown Photography.*

The moon gate and spillway connect to the dining room carp pool. Through the moon gate is the large entrance courtyard and copper entrance gate. The top of the inner garden walls is also copper. Enormous, irregular shaped, Pennsylvania bluestone slabs form the terrace surface. *Courtesy of Woodruff/Brown Photography.*

Detail view of dining room carp pool and stepping stones. A retaining wall was built on the existing rock ledge to form the pool edge. *Courtesy of Woodruff/Brown Photography.*

181

*Left:*
Main entrance courtyard has eight-inch thick stone slabs as a bridge to the front door. A walled courtyard was deemed necessary to keep herds of deer from eating the native shrubbery. Skylight in foreground gives light to the stairwell in the lower level. *Courtesy of Woodruff/Brown Photography.*

*Below:*
The walled garden gate and floating roof of copper are seen here. Heavy cedar timber construction and wrapped copper roof planks floating like shutter blades allow light to penetrate the structure. The gate and wall separate the exterior auto court from the interior walled garden with house and carp pools. *Courtesy of Woodruff/Brown Photography.*

The living room pavilion has sliding glass that recedes into pockets. It has a red cedar interior plank ceiling, white cedar walls, and French limestone floor with bluestone border that flows to the large irregular stones of the terrace and walkways. The channel contains water that flows around the pavilion. *Courtesy of Woodruff/Brown Photography.*

The Rockefeller Gardens of Seal Harbor, Mt. Desert Island, Maine, inspired this view through the moon gate to the inner walled garden. The main entrance bridge shown in the distance leads to the foyer entrance. The large glass bay/dormer contains a stairway leading to the master suite as well as to the lower-level moss and fern garden under the skylight. *Courtesy of Woodruff/Brown Photography.*

The kitchen has a custom bronze sink recessed below the Hawaiian granite countertop. The floors as well as the custom cabinetry are curly maple. Maple encased beams offset the elephant gray, basketweave grasscloth. *Courtesy of Jonathan Isleib.*

The stairs to the guest suite are designed to incorporate landings for the client's extensive sculpture collection. Maple stringers and bronze finished handrail incorporate the glass guards at the lower part of the rail. *Courtesy of Jonathan Isleib.*

The master suite has views overlooking the river and salt marshes and a walkout deck recessed into the roof. The fireplace has native stone surround and interior natural stucco finish. The ceiling of custom, milled, white aromatic cedar is shiplapped for the texture. *Courtesy of Jonathan Isleib.*

The master bath walls are aromatic white cedar; it has a French limestone floor with a border of elephant gray, fossil like polished stone. The teak countertop is two inches thick and the custom bowl is also of teak. The granite sink on the right has a limestone pedestal to the floor in order to block the shower splash. The shower (seen in the mirror) has a commanding view of the water. It has a limestone seat and walls; no curtain or glass partition is necessary. The floor is pitched to a six-foot continuous drain, and an appropriate plant controls any unwanted splash of the shower. *Courtesy of Jonathan Isleib.*

# Part Five

# S o m e t h i n g   i n   B e t w e e n

*Courtesy of D. Peter Lund.*

*Courtesy of D. Peter Lund.*

*Right:*
*Courtesy of D. Peter Lund.*

A farm by the sea. How bucolic is that? The wide driveway invites us to visit the house and the bay beyond. It also holds farm equipment. *Courtesy of D. Peter Lund.*

A downstairs bedroom with fireplace greets the tired visitor. *Courtesy of D. Peter Lund.*

Summers on the farm mean vegetables to harvest, cows to milk, eggs to collect, and falling stars to catch.
*Courtesy of D. Peter Lund.*

The antique farmhouse overlooks the quiet cove. *Courtesy of D. Peter Lund.*

The cove goes on forever. It means days of clamming, fishing, swimming, and boating. *Courtesy of D. Peter Lund.*

Connecticut Yankees still exist. This one overlooks the river with its constantly moving surface. *Courtesy of D. Peter Lund.*

The rising gold sun illuminates one of the formal rooms. *Courtesy of D. Peter Lund.*

Antiques fill this riverfront home.
*Courtesy of D. Peter Lund.*

You can play ping-pong and marvel at the constantly changing river scene at the same time. *Courtesy of D. Peter Lund.*

The path along the adjacent building leads to the water. *Courtesy of D. Peter Lund.*

The large rambling house overlooks the marshes teeming with life. *Courtesy of D. Peter Lund.*

Salt water marshes surround the house. *Courtesy of D. Peter Lund.*

The winterized porch is integrated with the natural world outside. *Courtesy of D. Peter Lund.*

Many species of birds make their home in the large marsh area. They bring the grounds alive with their bustling activity. *Courtesy of D. Peter Lund.*

A charming statue protects the small pond. *Courtesy of D. Peter Lund.*

"Down by the old millstream…" *Courtesy of D. Peter Lund.*

Despite its age, this old mill remains a tranquil refuge. *Courtesy of D. Peter Lund.*

The restored interior demonstrates principles of space and light that make living wonderful. *Courtesy of D. Peter Lund.*

The house exudes history and gracious living. *Courtesy of D. Peter Lund.*

Trickles of little brooks that appear only at magical places such as this ring like bells over the rocks. *Courtesy of D. Peter Lund.*

The bridge over the brook returns you to the 21st century. *Courtesy of D. Peter Lund.*

The river runs freely, and fish leap to catch the hovering mayfly. *Courtesy of D. Peter Lund.*

Here is a place where birds and bees stir summer air with wings of ease, and the river sparkles in the sun. *Courtesy of D. Peter Lund.*

Home from the sea, the sailor and his wife found this cape with its water views. *Courtesy of D. Peter Lund.*

Since the early 1900s, many artists have been attracted to the area by the beautiful trees, open meadows, tumbling streams, and great cliffs. The early renderings of the cove have been sold and resold as the artists have grown in stature. Artists still paint the busy cove scene today. *Courtesy of D. Peter Lund.*

The lake is the focal point of the house. From any spot in the house, the waves can be heard lapping at the rocks below. *Courtesy of D. Peter Lund.*

The road winds around stands of pines, birches, and stony bluffs. Then you come to the lake. *Courtesy of D. Peter Lund.*

The lake is an eternal mirror.
*Courtesy of D. Peter Lund.*

This home designed by O'Neil & Manion Architects P.A. has broad roof overhangs to shield it from the summer morning sun. They also provide a large protected porch with a view over the bay. *Courtesy of © Maxwell MacKenzie.*

The great room looks towards the water. Expansive walls of glass provide 180 degrees of view. *Courtesy of © Maxwell MacKenzie.*

**Opposing page:**

*Top left:*
The dining area of the great room looks to the Northeast.
*Courtesy of © Maxwell MacKenzie*

*Bottom left:*
The covered deck looks south. *Courtesy of © Maxwell MacKenzie.*

*Right:*
Great room with exposed heavy timber construction steps down into the dining area to provide unobstructed views to the water. *Courtesy of © Maxwell MacKenzie.*

The west elevation entry garden has a lovely trellis structure. *Courtesy of © Maxwell MacKenzie.*

207

The eastern elevation has a pool and trellis. The lawn is edged with wildflowers and sea grasses. *Courtesy of © Maxwell MacKenzie.*

Robert Oshatz, Architect, designed a studio with a sod roof that was built into the hillside to meet his clients' desire to blend into the surroundings. *Courtesy of Robert Oshatz, Architect.*

The sod roof and some of the boathouse portion of the structure are partially covered by the roof vegetation. *Courtesy of Robert Oshatz, Architect.*

The art studio is on the left. The study is tucked under the arching sod roof in the smaller curving section on the right. *Courtesy of Robert Oshatz, Architect.*

210

As you walk to the boathouse/studio, you see the sod roof hovering over the boathouse's wooden roof and the study beyond. *Courtesy of Robert Oshatz, Architect.*

This pathway leads to the structure's entrance. *Courtesy of Robert Oshatz, Architect.*

As you walk into the structure, the lake reappears. You can turn right and step down into the boathouse. *Courtesy of Robert Oshatz, Architect.*

To the right is the lake; to the left is the glass wall that has trapezoidal sliding doors to the studio and study. *Courtesy of Robert Oshatz, Architect.*

The working artist studio has wonderful natural light and high ceilings. *Courtesy of Robert Oshatz, Architect.*

The study area also has views of the water. *Courtesy of Robert Oshatz, Architect.*

To preserve wetlands and mature hardwoods, this house designed by Taylor & Burns is located at the narrow end of the property on a steep slope between road and shore. The house parallels the shoreline and the sloping grade, offering a broad open face to the lake. © *Greg Premru*.

The exterior presents two different faces. The formal, private north side fronting the road has a stick-work arch entrance and a few small windows on cedar shingle walls. © *Greg Premru*.

The south side opens dramatically towards the lake. The broad eaves and deck anchor the house to the shoreline. Generous windows welcome the sun and the panoramic views. © *Greg Premru*.

Grouped windows and glazed doors allow the main spaces to flow outward to the deck and the lake. © *Greg Premru.*

The stick-work on the entry arch frames the lawn. © *Greg Premru.*

The stone fireplace is the focus of the tall living room. Its chimney links the three levels of the house. © *Greg Premru.*

The second-floor balcony running behind the chimney is amply lit by a row of windows. Bedrooms at either end tuck under the roof dormers. © *Greg Premru.*

Beyond the entry hall and staircase, the back hall leads out to the screen porch. © *Greg Premru.*

This spectacular lakeside home is sited on a small island. *Courtesy of Topsider.*

Topsider's large, open style floor plan makes this spacious combined kitchen, dining, and living area ideal for large family gatherings. *Courtesy of Topsider.*

A small informal dining area and open stairway are excellent examples of the flexibility of the design. *Courtesy of Topsider.*

An intimate guest suite opens onto a deck and the lake. *Courtesy of Topsider.*

Designed with plenty of deck space, a sunroom, and screened porch, this Topsider home with its pedestal design fits snugly into the steep hillside. *Courtesy of Topsider.*

The kitchen, dining, and living areas flow together in this open style floor plan. *Courtesy of Topsider.*

The rustic elegance of a stone fireplace dominates this cozy, light-bathed living space. *Courtesy of Topsider.*

An attached sunroom captures the day's end over the lake. *Courtesy of Topsider.*

This Topsider home is literally built at the water's edge. *Courtesy of Topsider.*

Vaulted, exposed beam ceilings are found in every room. *Courtesy of Topsider.*

A modern galley kitchen adds to the seaside charm. *Courtesy of Topsider.*

Wide and expansive decks connect to provide sequestered views of the beach below. *Courtesy of Topsider.*

A modern, open style kitchen and dining area have all the amenities. *Courtesy of Topsider.*

One of several contemporary living spaces opens onto extraordinary views. *Courtesy of Topsider.*

A secluded walkway leads to this hidden Topsider home. *Courtesy of Topsider.*

The dining area is literally set in the trees, blending the inside and outside in seamless harmony. *Courtesy of Topsider.*

Weber Murphy Fox designed a home in an upscale residential subdivision on a lot overlooking the lake. *Courtesy of Art Becker.*

The formal entrance to the house is through an entry court. *Courtesy of Art Becker.*

The entrance portico provides a wind-sheltered outdoor space, which extends the season in the sun. *Courtesy of Art Becker.*

The foyer leads to the main stairwell. *Courtesy of Art Becker.*

The two-story living room has a balcony/library at the south end of the space under a large round window. Circular windows bring light into library and living room. *Courtesy of Art Becker.*

227

The second floor contains guest bedrooms and the master bedroom suite. *Courtesy of Art Becker.*

The master bath overlooks the lake. *Courtesy of Art Becker.*

This lakeside house designed by Zaik/Miller drops down and around a rocky site, working its way among the outcroppings. *Courtesy of Art Hupey.*

The flow of interior spaces gives a sophisticated feeling. *Courtesy of Stephen Cridland.*

The rooms have skylights and high window projections, which provide natural light. *Courtesy of Stephen Cridland.*

The fine detailing uses natural woods, combined with stonework and sculpture and ceramic work. *Courtesy of Stephen Cridland.*

Zimmerman Architects designed the open-plan house to take advantage of all the natural features of the site. The lake front elevation is viewed across the cove from the opposite shore. *Courtesy of Hope Zimmerman AIA.*

*Left:*
The street front elevation evokes the feeling of the original summer bungalow, which had been removed to build a new, three bedroom, year-round residence on a sloping lakefront property.
*Courtesy of Hope Zimmerman AIA.*

Use of multilevel decks allows for greater enjoyment of the lake from many areas of the house, including the second-floor master bedroom. Decks can be found everywhere. *Courtesy of Hope Zimmerman AIA.*

The inviting front entry has a view to the lake beyond. *Courtesy of Hope Zimmerman AIA.*

The client wanted to be able to experience the lake from inside the house. With the open floor plan, the lake is visible from almost every room in the house, whether directly or through another room. *Courtesy of Hope Zimmerman AIA.*

The stair landing affords a view of the open first-floor kitchen, the second-floor loft, and, of course, the lake. The open stairway allows you to see through and around. *Courtesy of Hope Zimmerman AIA.*

The loft, with its sixteen foot cathedral ceiling and built-in floor-to-ceiling bookcases, overlooks the sunken living room and dining room below and the lake. The view of the lake gives it a quiet, reflective setting, while maintaining its connection with the first floor below. *Courtesy of Hope Zimmerman AIA.*

The many jogs in this house help blur the distinction between inside and outside because your view to the lake from many of the doors and windows includes a glimpse of other parts of the house. *Courtesy of Hope Zimmerman AIA.*

The living room has a cathedral ceiling. Here, you see it with the curved stair landing and a glimpse of the lake beyond the deck. *Courtesy of Hope Zimmerman AIA.*

# Meet the Architects
## and Designers

**Albertsson Hansen Architecture, Ltd.**, a residential architecture firm, located in Minneapolis, is known for its excellence in design, detail, and attentive service. Projects include new residences, remodeling, cabins, and residential outbuildings.

1005 West Franklin Ave., Suite 5, Minneapolis, Minnesota 55405; (612) 823-0233; www.aharchitecture.com; email: info@aharchitecture.com.

Practicing in Sedona, Arizona, and Telluride, Colorado, **Eric Brandt Architect** has nearly 20 years' experience designing and building custom residential and commercial projects in outstanding natural environments. The firm strives to be highly responsive to clients and their projects, with great attention to details.

P.O. Box 1014, Sedona, Arizona 86339; (928) 203-9918; www.BrandtArchitect.com.

**DiPrima Fine Homes** have been building award winning, custom homes in Brevard County, Florida, for over 40 years. The firm offers homes ranging from intimate, quality built villas and townhouses to luxurious, multi-million dollar estates. With the growth and experience of the company, the DiPrima name has become synonymous with integrity, competence, and quality.

1199 So. Patrick Dr., Satellite Beach, Florida 32937; (321) 777-2500; www.diprima.com.

**CBT/Childs Bertman Tseckares Inc.**, a professional design firm, provides services in architecture, site planning, and urban design. Founded in Boston in 1967, its practice includes the design of office, residential, academic, civic, and hospitality buildings, and a variety of interior spaces. The firm has received over 120 awards, recognizing the excellence and creativity in its design of new buildings and the preservation of existing structures.

110 Canal St., Boston, Massachusetts 02114-1805; (617) 262-4354; www.cbtarchitects.com.

**Interdesign Limited**'s philosophy focuses strongly on the project's natural environment. "The design objective is to blend the structure with nature using the colors and textures of the site, integrating the natural contours, trees, rocks, views, and solar orientation. These factors guide the design process including the interior design, which is an integral part of the architectural whole. Our designs incorporate traditional ideas with contemporary ways of living by drawing on multicultural, traditional forms of enduring beauty and adapting them to the client's lifestyle. We strive to achieve a sense of timelessness while creating an exciting, sculptural living environment that is in harmony with nature."

101 Shore Road, P.O. Box 250, Old Lyme, Connecticut 06371; (860) 434-8083; email@interdesign-ltd.com.

**Arthur Cotton Moore FAIA** travels (67 countries), lectures, serves on design juries, paints (solo shows here and abroad), designed an award-winning furniture series, and writes (*The Powers of Preservation*, McGraw-Hill). An internationally recognized architect, his work has received over seventy design awards and appeared in over 2,000 publications.

4533 Benoni Point Rd., Royal Oak, Maryland 21662; email: pmoore@goeaston.net.

Established in 1983, **Muse Architects** has extensive experience in residential, institutional, commercial, and urban design projects. It has received more than 80 design awards, including those from the National, Washington, Maryland, and Baltimore Chapters of the AIA, the National Trust for Historic Preservation, and the Masonry Institute. More than 125 architectural books and periodicals, including *Architectural Digest, House Beautiful, The American Home,* and *Design for Living,* have reviewed its work.

5630 Connecticut Ave., NW, Washington, D.C. 20015; (202) 966-6266; www.musearchitects.com.

Founded in 1977, **O'Neil & Manion Architects P.A**. is a full service architectural firm in Bethesda, Maryland. The firm's history of developing distinct and creative solutions to projects is recognized with numerous design awards and features in *Architectural Digest, Architecture, Builder, Qualified Remodeler, Washingtonian Magazine, Southern Living,* and other publications.

6931 Arlington Rd., Suite 306, Bethesda, Maryland 20814; (301) 654-7004; email: wcm@oneilandmanion.com.

**Oregon South Shore Contractors** started building New England style homes and luxury, beach front condominiums in 1995. Innovative building techniques like the use of Formtech™ brand insulating concrete walls create incredible comfort, 100% dry rot protection, triple fire protection, superior earthquake protection, and six times better noise reduction than traditional wood walls.

6225 SW Arbor, Newport, Oregon 97366; (541) 867-4545; email: scott@quality-concrete.com.

**Robert Oshatz, Architect,** states, "I have developed strong working relationships with the clients I have served. These relationships are based on the understanding that architecture is the synthesis of logic and emotion and the exploration and fulfillment of my client's dreams, fantasies, and realities. I view architecture as a problem-solving profession…the starting point of any project is the client's program. So, the first step is to divide the program into its functional requirements,

technical space allocations, and relationships. To succeed, it must also embody the clients' emotional and spiritual needs while capturing their vision."

PO Box 19091, Portland, Oregon 97219; (505) 635-4243; www.oshatz.com; email: robert@oshatz.com.

Nestled on 5,200 acres of classic Vermont countryside, **Quechee Lakes Development Company** is a community filled with traditions, customs, and valued friendships. It's far from the bustle of city life, but surrounded by a wide array of activities, shops, restaurants, museums, and historic sites. "Quechee Lakes is a place where you and your family can connect with nature, as well as with your neighbors."

176 Waterman Hill Rd., Quechee, Vermont 05059; (888) 592-2224 or (802) 295-5100; email: info@quecheelakes.com.

**Don Ritz AIA** practices in the Boston area. He specializes in residential renovations and additions as well as new construction in coastal locations. Mr. Ritz believes traditional architecture done correctly still holds much worth in the modern world and that a small project benefiting from careful attention to detail can be more rewarding to a client than a larger but ill-designed project.

21 Q St., Hull, Massachusetts 02045; (781) 925-2881; email: Dritz21Q@aol.com.

**Siemasko + Verbridge** is a full-service architectural, interior design, and space planning firm. The firm's projects encompass residential, corporate, commercial, and institutional design, inclusive of both new construction and renovation work. It prides itself on a powerful team approach and high caliber design.

126 Dodge St., Beverly, Massachusetts 01915; (978) 927-3745; www.svdesign.com.

**Clay Benjamin Smook AIA** is a registered architect and a graduate of New York Institute of Technology and Harvard University Graduate School of Design. He has been designing waterfront homes for over 20 years. His projects have appeared in *Fine Homebuilding, Builder Magazine,* and on HGTV. He practices architecture and urban design in the Boston area.

139 Elliot Ave., North Quincy, Massachusetts 02171; (617) 901-7669; email: smook@comcast.net.

**Taylor & Burns Architects** is an award-winning design firm located in Boston, Massachusetts, specializing in residential and small-scale institutional work. Partners Robert Taylor and Carol Burns are integrally involved in each project. Their designs highlight beauty through a fresh take on familiar things: walls, rooms, windows, light.

58 Winter St., Boston, Massachusetts 02108; (617) 357-5335; www.taylorburns.com.

**Thielsen Architects, Inc. P.S.** is a vibrant design-oriented firm that is committed to creating distinctive environments. It believes that thoughtful spatial organization and sensitivity to the site and natural light achieve sensible design solutions. The firm strives to design architecture that will remain as functional and beautiful over time as it is today.

720 Market St., Suite C, Kirkland, Washington 98033; (425) 828-0333; www.thielsenarchitects.com.

**Topsider Homes** are designed for waterfront living…with plenty of deck space, vaulted, exposed-beam ceilings, and breathtaking panoramic views throughout. A unique pedestal design also makes an ideal alternative to coastal area pilings and provides the perfect building solution for severely sloping lake front sites.

P.O. Box 1490, Clemmons, North Carolina 27012; (866) 867-9300 or (336)-766-9300; www.topsider.com; email: topsider@topsider.com.

One of the founders of **Weber Murphy Fox,** Herman Weber has personally designed most of the firm's major complex projects and has provided overall leadership. He believes that many waterfront homes are designed around furniture groupings, which turn their back on the wonderful water views. The living spaces in his houses are designed to provide a triple focal point: fireplace, TV, and water view. In addition, window seats are incorporated in a variety of configurations to invite people to curl up, read a book, and enjoy the water views through the changing seasons.

3230 West Lake Rd., Erie, Pennsylvania (814) 836-1515; www.webermurphyfox.com; email: hweber@webermurphyfox.com.

**Zaik/Miller Associates,** founded in 1966 by Saul Zaik FAIA and James Miller AIA in Portland, Oregon, has been influential in the formation of a unique, northwest, contemporary style architecture. This regional approach integrates homes to site and natural landscape with the use of native materials and landforms. The beauty and simplicity of their design forms spring from people use and function and relate to views, sun, and weather orientation.

2340 Northwest Thurman, Suite 201, Portland, Oregon 97210; (503) 222-9158; www.zaikmiller.com.

Twin sisters Faith and Hope Zimmerman (**Zimmerman Architects**) are delighted to practice architecture together in Morris County, New Jersey. After pursuing individual career paths in engineering and fine arts, they found themselves reunited in architecture. Several years ago, Zimmerman Architects made a deliberate decision to concentrate on custom residential projects because those were the clients who really appreciated how much they put their hearts into their projects.

One East Main St. Denville, New Jersey 07834; (973) 625-4001; email: zimarch@nac.net.